Android Development Guide for the Newbie

Tips & Tricks to Making Great Apps

By: Jason Hunter

I0004549

PUBLISHERS NOTES

Disclaimer

This publication is intended to provide helpful and informative material. It is not intended to diagnose, treat, cure, or prevent any health problem or condition, nor is intended to replace the advice of a physician. No action should be taken solely on the contents of this book. Always consult your physician or qualified health-care professional on any matters regarding your health and before adopting any suggestions in this book or drawing inferences from it.

The author and publisher specifically disclaim all responsibility for any liability, loss or risk, personal or otherwise, which is incurred as a consequence, directly or indirectly, from the use or application of any contents of this book.

Any and all product names referenced within this book are the trademarks of their respective owners. None of these owners have sponsored, authorized, endorsed, or approved this book.

Always read all information provided by the manufacturers' product labels before using their products. The author and publisher are not responsible for claims made by manufacturers.

Paperback Edition

Manufactured in the United States of America

DEDICATION

This book is dedicated to the persons that strive to be leaders in the field of technology. To those who strive to discover new and innovative ways for things to get done. The advancement of technology will only help us to function better in our fast paced world.

TABLE OF CONTENTS

CHAPTER 1- ANDROID- WHAT IS IT?

When looking at smartphones, the term "Android" is always going to come up. A lot of people are familiar with iPhones and the iOS operating system. However, a lot of people still don't know exactly what Android is. What is Android?

Android happens to be the most widespread and popular mobile phone operating system in the world. It is also a very popular operating system for tablets. Different devices run different operating systems. A PC usually runs Windows; a MacBook runs Mac OS; an iPhone runs iOS; a Windows phone runs Windows Mobile 8. Depending on what kind of device you're talking about, the list can go on and on. Android was developed and is currently run by Google. What makes Android unique is that Google gives Android away to developers that want to use it on their devices. This is in stark contrast to a company like Apple. Apple is in complete and utter control of iOS. No other manufacturer is allowed to use Apple. Even if one wanted to, they would be forced to be a hefty fee. Google gives Android away for free. This is the reason why Android is on so many different devices compared to competitors. Samsung uses Android; HTC uses Android; Sony uses

Android; Dell uses Android; ASUS uses Android; Lenovo uses Android. The list goes on nearly forever.

Android was founded in Palo Alto, California in the year 2003. It was first created by Andy Rubin, Rich Sears, Chris White, and Rich Miner. Google bought the company in 2005 and was poised to enter the mobile phone market. The very first Android phone was developed by HTC and was known as the HTC Dream or the T-Mobile G1. The phone was released in 2008 and was the first phone to try to go head-to-head with the extremely popular iPhone and BlackBerry smartphones. The phone was released to a good reception and the Android product line only grew from there.

In 2010, Google launched the Nexus series of devices. Nexus devices became popular because they would almost always coincide with the release of the next version of the Android operating system. Nexus devices were, and continue to be, the first phones to get access to the newest version of Android.

Since the beginning of Android, there have been many updates to the operating system. These updates are mostly used to improve functionality. They have also been used to change the visual appeal of Android over the years. The first versions of Android look quite different from the newest versions. Froyo was the first version of Android, followed by Gingerbread, Honeycomb, Ice Cream Sandwich, Jelly Bean, and KitKat.

Since its inception, Android has grown to become the most popular operating system for mobile phones. This is likely due to the lower cost of Android handsets when compared to the iPhone. In addition to that, there are also many more options available for those on the Android platform. All in all, Android has grown quite a bit from its humble origins in Silicon Valley.

Established in November of 2007, the Android alliance team is a consortium of over 84 technology companies that gave birth to the android system. This consortium comprises of major firms like: Google, HTC. T-Mobile, Dell, Motorola, Texas Instruments, LG Electronics, Sprint, Nvidia and others. The membership involves companies coming in as manufacturers of the hardware and software for mobile devices. It also includes companies offering network and mobile communication technology.

The idea behind this alliance is an emphasis on open-source applications; applications that can be built and used by builders of mobile devices without necessarily having to buy or procure the license. The Android system, the main flagship of this alliance was officially released on a mobile device in August 2008, through HTC Dream G1 T-Mobile device.

An important thing that the Android alliance has achieved is the provision of a platform where Android is a common operating system. This system is available to a wide conglomerate of technology providers who are only left to focus on building middleware and end-user applications. The alliance maintains a shared repository that allows developers to build on both existing and expected technology. Sharing of new development practices through open codes and development documentations ensures new programs are easily tweaked to scale into evolving technology.

The main objective of the Open Handset Alliance is to promote the innovation of applications and mobile devices that have increased openness. This, according to them will allow rapid innovation as they build on existing technology. The emphasis is to discourage "re-invention" of the wheel or a scenario where every company builds technology from scratch instead of enhancing existing innovation.

The alliance has translated into low cost and high-tech mobile devices produced at shorter innovation time spans. The other important fact is that, when technology has a common platform, then it is easy for different manufactures to cross-sell their supporting technologies across different devices.

If a technology company innovates an application that gives users a certain capability, they do not have to build an "add-on" to every operating system under different mobile devices. The fact that these devices have a common Android system, then are able to use the same original application without getting tailor-made/add-ons for the different systems. This quality is easily refereed to simplified integration. Because Android system was developed specifically for Mobile devices, and it being an open-source system (which means it is free and accessible to any member of this alliance), manufactures of handsets can focus on building the best devices that make use of the operating system and by that focus on mobile device innovations.

It is important to observe that the open-handset alliance is a hint to what the technology markets have already leaned to. The development of devices, that more often than not, are able to share information and connect at different levels. When mobile device pioneers started, they leaned more towards exclusivity. Today, the most important feature is inclusiveness. There is no doubt that large companies that have stayed away from the alliance are either re-thinking their strategies or establishing similar open-ware niche.

CHAPTER 2- THE DIFFERENT TYPES OF ANDROID APPLICATIONS

Android Applications

For those who are delving into the Android operating system, it's important to remember how Android applications work and the different types of Android applications. For one, an Android package is commonly referred to as an .apk. Files with the .apk suffix comprise of all the different contents that is needed for the application. For instance, if you download the .apk for a gallery application that's only on the HTC One, you could download this .apk file and get that same gallery application on your Nexus 5. This is what makes the Android operating system so unique when compared to iOS or Windows Mobile.

When it comes to apps, there are different types of apps that perform different kinds of actions. These are the types of apps that can be developed for Android:

Games

Games are exactly what you think they are. There are many different games on the Google Play Store and they all serve a different purpose. There are games from just about every genre imaginable. There are RPGs, action games, strategy games, racing games, and many other. Almost all Android games utilize the touch screen. All in all, the sky is the limit when it comes to developing Android games. A lot of Android phones have enough processing power and memory to run fairly high quality games.

Widgets

Widgets are quite unique to the Android operating system. Widgets refer to different applications that can be placed directly on the home screen. Widgets are mainly used to display information in real time. For instance, there is a battery manager widget that will update the user on how much battery he/she has. All of this happens in real time. For example, if the user sees that he/she has P of their battery left, when they look a few minutes later, it's going to update to H. There's no reason to reload the application, it will do so automatically. This is entirely different from normal apps in which the app needs to be manually reloaded in order to receive new information.

Applications

The rest are just known as "applications." With that being said, applications are very broad in scope. Anything can be considered an application. There are banking applications; there are social networking applications; there are email applications. This list goes on and on. Applications are mainly just meant to provide a certain service or perform a task. These tasks usually require what's known as "permissions." For example, there could be an app developed that turns an Android phone into a flashlight. Launching the app will get "permission" from the camera software to turn on the flash. Once approved (this can be done manually or automatically) the camera flash will turn on. Or a social networking app can request "permission" to view the names of the contacts in your phone as a means to connect you with your friends on that particular social networking site.

All in all, there are a few different applications on the Android operating system and they all behave a bit differently. Knowing how they work is essential to developing for Android.

Android Activities

Android activities are components of an application that provide screens to the users so that they can interact when they wish to achieve a motive, for instance – viewing a map, sending an email, taking a picture or dialing a number on the phone. Every individual activity is provided with a window for drawing its UI (user interface). In most cases, the window's size is such that it fits the screen perfectly. However, depending on the UI, it could float above other windows or it could be smaller than the screen.

Activity Task – A collection of various activities that a user comes in touch with when they need to perform a certain job is called a task.

Activity Stack – This is an arrangement of activities in the form of a stack (called 'back stack'). The order in which the activities are opened is the order in which they are arranged in the back stack.

In an application, there are various activities that are loosely connected to each other. When an application is launched by the user for the first time, the "main activity" is seen by the user. As different actions are performed for different requirements, the related activities are started. When one activity begins, the previous activity ends or stops.

However, the "back stack" is the place where that previous stopped activity is kept alive by the application. Thus, whenever a new activity is started, it instantly takes the focus of the user and is pushed in the back stack. The mechanism of the back stack is simple – last in, first out. When the "back" button is pressed by the user after finishing a particular activity, it gets removed or destroyed (popped) from the back stack and the previous activity starts again.

Activity States – Essentially, an activity has 3 states:

- **Running or Active State** – When the activity is placed on top of the stack, it is considered to be active as it is present in the screen's foreground.
- **Paused State** – This state is achieved when the activity is not running and has lost focus. However, you can still see the activity because it is visible. It is under a non-full sized activity which is essentially transparent and has user focus. The activity would still be alive in its paused state but if the memory is low, it will be killed.
- **Stopped State** – When another activity completely obscures an activity, even when it retains member information and all states, it is a stopped state. When the memory is needed by the system somewhere else, the stopped activity, which is not visible to the user, will be killed.

There are methods of lifecycle call back in an activity which performs the function of notifying an activity when it has been stopped by the user. There are various call back methods, depending on the state of the activity. A stopped or paused activity can be dropped from the memory any time by the system by either killing its process or asking it to finish. When the same activity is started again, the process is repeated again.

Chapter 3- The Android User Interface Design

Those who delve into Android application design should have an idea of what the design language is for Android apps. Since Android is an open source operating system, this allows a lot of developers to do almost whatever they want in regards to application design. As mentioned in Chapter 1, this is in stark contrast with iOS which has a very specific and mandatory design language that developers must follow. With that being said, it's important for Android developers to follow the vision that Google has for the Android user interface. This makes the application more attractive and people will be more inclined to use it. There are many different criteria that make up Google's envisioned ideas for the Android user interface design.

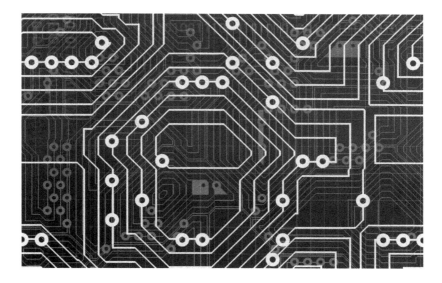

Flatness

Flatness has become the new big thing in the Android user interface. A lot of apps that are optimized for Android are very flat. This means that buttons and menus don't have a three-dimensional appearance. "Buttons" don't actually look like buttons. The design language mostly started with Android 4.0 Ice Cream Sandwich and has become more ingrained in the Android UI ever since.

Optimization for On-Screen Navigation Bars

A lot of Android phones are moving to having on-screen navigation buttons as opposed to physical or capacitive buttons. Samsung is lagging behind in this regard, but it's only a matter of time before they switch over as well. With that being said, applications that make use a full screen have to take these navigation bars into consideration. When viewing media, it's important that the user gets to make use of the screen real estate of the entire phone. Google added what's known as "Immersive Mode" as a means to make this navigation bars disappear.

Navigation Bar on the Left

Very common to Android is a navigation bar that extends from the left. Typically, this bar allows users to navigate to different areas of the application. This has become a staple in Android UI design and is a very handy tool. It is usually accessed by swiping from the left edge of the screen to the right. There is also usually a little button on the top corner of the screen as a means to display the navigation bar.

#HoloYolo

Holo is the name of the "theme" for the Android UI. There is a Holo Light theme and a Holo Dark theme. It's always good to give an option for whether users want to use Light or Dark. Light themes are better for users who have a device with an LCD display.

Jason Hunter

Meanwhile, Dark themes are better for those who have a device with an AMOLED display.

Color Palette

Typically speaking, blue has been the color palette for the Android operating system. With that being said, ever since the Android 4.4 KitKat update, it seems that white accents are the new standard. However, the text in the dialer is still blue on most Android devices. Either color would work.

All in all, these are the major components of the Android user interface design. It isn't particularly strict in regards to what developers can choose to do. However, aligning with the common user interface gives users a more refined and consistent experience.

CHAPTER 4- ANDROID DEVELOPMENT FRAMEWORK AND LIBRARIES

Android Development Framework

Since Android has become the world's most popular mobile application platform, many developers have been drawn on board. Many new developers will need to understand what they can get from an Android development framework. This is effectively a system that will enable developers to bring together solutions to suit their needs. Some developers will understandably be impressed by the sheer amount of utility that they can get when they opt to test out this program. Developers will have to decide what kinds of features that they need to get. This could be an excellent project for a development team that might now understand how the programs could be used.

First, it will be important to identify the application that people want to customize throughout the year. This is part of the reason why most development teams will appreciate finding a specialty framework. Many of them will use JavaScript and a few other unique features when people test them out for themselves soon. Most of these frameworks will use some kind of programming language, so developers should identify these resources soon. This could help development teams improve the overall expertise that they tend to get when they check out these systems for themselves.

There are actually some cross platform development frameworks that people could opt to use. This could be especially important for developers who want to publish their work across a few different types of mobile operating systems. There are actually many that will work for both the Android OS and the iOS trading platforms soon. Phone Gap and Dojo Mobile are two excellent options for customers out on the market. This could be an excellent resource for anyone who wants to increase the number of times the program itself is downloaded by users. Expanding across platforms can take some programming flexibility, but the investment will be well worth it to many.

Some development teams may need to secure some ancillary development framework tools. These can be used to test different types of component features of the apps the teams are creating. They can use these framework tools to gauge how the application might be perceived by the public. Developers should opt to use Testdroid to evaluate some of the different features that they can see through here. DroidDraw will make it surprisingly simple for people to test out the GUI design for themselves. This could prove to be one of the most valuable component features that everyone may want to use.

Finally, most developers will want to check out how they can get Android ready frameworks for their programs. Basic4Android and Corona SDK are immediately useful for people who need to improve the results that they want to see. Most customers will appreciate the sheer simplicity of how they can download these frameworks and get started. Many of them are also fairly lightweight and will feature a small overall file size. This means that they will tend to work on a wide variety of different types of platforms over time.

Android Development Libraries

Applications programming interfaces (API's) directs/manages the behavior of applications as they interact with each other. Since the Android system is an open source platform, many application developers are working daily to ensure that; first, the technology they build is able to work on the android system, but more importantly, the technology achieves an optimal performance.

By optimal performance, the reference is to make sure the android system is working together with the other application and provides the user the best/intended outcome. Once APIs and other application aspects are coded, their use for different developers under a similar platform like Android is possible and beneficial. The Android Libraries is a collection of such API's and related codes.

It is easy to assume that all developers will easily build compatible applications/devices, but without such developers having standard references to how the android system interacts with different applications, it might be tasking and take unnecessarily long. This is where the android development libraries come in. These libraries consist of code collections, different level APIs and other android development tools. In that way, android based devices can use applications from different developers and yet achieve standard compatibility and optimality.

The Android development Libraries also give developers a centralized collection of codes and knowledge. It also acts as a subtle standard setting platform since developers are obliged to use the different android APIs for enhancing or fully building their applications.

With the increased popularity of Android platforms, developers are able to use a centralized library to hasten their development efforts. This is because the library offers platforms to enhance the widespread adoption of tools and applications developed within the Android APIs quality. Example; Developers building tools within an English speaking country can easily incorporate codes and tools offered under Android Libraries to easily avail their products in other languages. Another example, is standard codes like developing the capability of an android developer's application to share information with another android based application.

The Android development libraries also provide a knowledge database that offers prospective developers an opportunity to acquire basic to advanced knowledge on android apps development. In such a forum, young enthusiasts and wanna-be developers have an opportunity to create, not from scratch but an already existing body of codes and APIs. This substantially cuts application development cost and time. It also makes it easy for business analysts and other need-solution architects to easily map clearer IT-business solutions.

Since Android is the most popular mobile device platform, and daily, a million android powered devices get turned on for the first time. The need for a reliable market place for different application tools is grand. Applications for different people, different environments, markets, languages, needs, devices and the list goes on. Such a need requires a freelance, open source development lab, where developers can share all and every information, share development tools and use the shortest periods of time to develop the best of applications. There is one place for such kind of innovation and collaboration and Android Development Libraries the only such place.

CHAPTER 5- NATIVE ANDROID APPLICATIONS

Although the default language used for Android development is Java, programmers tend to have their own code preferences which aren't always Java. Additionally, programmers will have already begun coding in another language and want to apply the work they've already completed for Android development. Both of these are situations where a Native Android Application would come into play to extend the options in the coding libraries that are available to developers.

These Native Android Applications allow developers the ability to manage different aspects of an Android operating system application through the use of more than just the Java programming language. This way Native Android Applications can be utilized with the help of an Android Native Development Kit (NDK). A variety of different devices can be used with an NDK including Windows, certain Mac systems, and Linux systems.

Essentially what an NDK can do is provide helpful bits and pieces to develop richer, more intricate content by using various types of code rather than just Java. By providing headers and an extensive library, you will have the opportunity to utilize more elements with the help of other programming languages. You will be allowed to package these bits and pieces and then upload them and incorporate them into the rest of your code for Android.

A statement from Google endorses a program called Eclipse, the typical plugin used for developers to aid in Android development. Eclipse is what is called an Integrated Development Environment, or IDE, and serves as a platform for debugging and graphical layout use. Google touts Eclipse as a reliable, safe, and user-friendly program, and a great resource for creating future programs for Android development. In fact, Google has recently released a new program entitled Android Studio that was created with the help of Eclipse. Eventually, Google plans on eventually replacing Eclipse with Android Studio as the official IDE for Android.

The Android development tools are easily accessible and nearly completely free of charge. There is no charge for the development tools, and applications may be freely added to compatible devices. To get an app from the Google Play store, you must first sign up for an account to enable publishing which includes a $25 fee. Getting apps in the Google Play store is significantly easier than for other platforms. When your application has been submitted to Google, it is checked briefly for possible threats. Generally, the application becomes available to the public in less than a day.

Publishing an app with Google Play is a great option to get started on your own development work. Because it is so easy to get your creations approved, you can immediately have published work to recommend yourself to others as well as personally stretch yourself to see what you are capable of. Utilizing Native Android Applications can help you on your way by allowing you to diversify your tool set by creating an opportunity for you to make more intricate applications with the use of other programming languages to add complexity to the capabilities of Java.

Eclipse For Android

Many Android applications are in existence only because of eclipse which is an open source integrated development environment for Java. Eclipse is the central place where the application software is created and structured and is supported by many of its own lifestyle cycles. As the only producer of Android and its products, Google is the only one to support it. It has also created the Android Development Tools Plugin for Eclipse and also has a device management built into the tools too. Basically, this means that you cannot single out building Java programs, but you can innovate Android-oriented codes. The testing of Eclipse is supported by virtual devices that allow users to see how their codes will run in the standard versions of any particular Android device. An Android Development Tool is pretty much a plugin for the Eclipse integrated development environment that is made to give users a more powerful integrated environment. This is how many people build Android applications too. The Android Development Tool is extending the capabilities of Eclipse to allow app builders to swiftly create and set up new Android jobs, projects, applications, and add components based on the framework of Android. This development tool also debugs your apps using many of the other Android tools and can even extract your files in order to help you distribute your application. The developers of Eclipse made the development tools a lot faster, and recommend everyone use it to get started. It provides the tools, customizes editors, and debugs your output pane. This tool will give you an awesome boost in helping you develop your Android apps.

The Android software Eclipse started back in 2001 with IBM more as a replacement for visual Age family of integrated development environment type of products. Google had an attraction to this as it was in an extensible plugin system and could be moved to go with extra functioning abilities. These abilities are also supported by third-party plug-ins. The founders of Eclipse used Ericsson, HP, Intel, IBM, and many other major technology software producers. This is all maintained by their foundation which is a non-profit supported corporation that helps Eclipse main projects and assists in proving an open source community and a system of free services and products. They build Android projects by downloading several plugins such as Java, Android, and the plugin for Eclipse.

Android offers a customized version of the plugin for the Eclipse integrated development environment and if you need to install it you can download it from eclipse.org under the "downloads" section of the website. Eclipse can be used to develop programs in other programming languages and can be used to develop packages for other software. The Eclipse software development kit has the ability to install plugins for its platform. This is also free and it runs under GNU Class path which implements free software for Java programming. There is a lot to be excited about in application development today because of Eclipse.

CHAPTER 6- ANDROID SOFTWARE DEVELOPMENT KITS

Android SDK stands for Android Software Development Kit. Android SDKs were created to give developers the opportunity to create software for Android operating systems. The kits offers tools that will allow developers to innovate within the spectrum of the operating system. This chapter provides an introduction to what SDKs are, what's included in an SDK, how SDKs can benefit developers, and where one can find an SDK.

Each Android SDK contains a variety of essential materials. These include debugging tools, an emulator, Android application program interface (API) information, tutorials for the operating system the kit is for, and other relevant information and tools that will assist developers.

Whenever a new version of the Android operating system is released, an SDK for that version of the program is released simultaneously. This ensures that developers will have the ability to create new programs with the latest features and nuances of the system. It also means that apps and programs that were created under a different operating system can be updated to be more functional in the newest operating system.

Each new Android SDK must be downloaded by the user on a device that is compatible with Android technology. Some of the operating systems that support Android include Linux products, Windows XP and up, and even Mac X from version 10.4.9 and on. Some add-ons from other creators can also be used.

One of the greatest uses of an Android SDK is to actually write code for Android programs. While this a great capability of the SDK, many people are more inclined to use something called an integrated development environment (often shortened to IDE) to

Jason Hunter

write in conjunction with the SDK. Some popular IDEs that many find useful include NetBeans, Eclipse, and IntelliJ.

The Android SDKs provide valuable samples of code within the interface so that programmers can learn about how code should look within the system and get a feel for how their work will look within the operating system. The documents provided also come with excellent references for your own work. These tools are invaluable for learning firsthand what will work within the operating system and teach developers how to put their best foot forward in the context of the new system.

In fact, SDKs are sometimes referred to by developers as coding libraries. This is because there are so many examples of coding provided in the SDKs. This makes an SDK a rich resource for inspiration as well as a great learning tool.

You can download the newest SDKs for Android directly with Android. On their website, Android provides a link to download their ADT bundle for windows. All developers have to do to have this invaluable information at their fingertips is follow Android's simple instructions for downloading the package with their compatible device. Android prepares any developer for an easy start by providing the SDK along with Eclipse and its plug-ins, basic platform tools for the new operating system, and an emulator. This easy to download package is the best bet for any developer.

The Android SDK Manager

For a developer who is looking to create applications for the Android-based operating system, it is necessary to obtain the Android SDK Manager. This SDK manager provides all of the necessary tools, programming features and updates required for a developer to create such an application. There are different components of the Android SDK Manager, so it is essential for a designer to know all of the different features and what it is able to do for them and their development capabilities.

The Android SDK Manager separates every single platform component, so designers are able to download only what they need. There might be some components of the Android SDK Manager that a particular designer does not need, so they might not feel obligated to download it. However, there are other tools that are required, as the application is not going to work if these particular applications are not currently running on the computer system used to design the application. The Android SDK Manager runs inside of either the Eclipse or Android Studio design platform. This platform makes it easier to create the applications specifically for Android.

In order to locate the different programming tools available on the Android SDK Manager, it is rather straight forward. In the Eclipse software, all you need to do is choose the "Window" tab, and then "Android SDK Manager". This shows all of the available components available in the Android SDK Manager. For the Android Studio software, you need to click "Tools," "Android" and finally "SDK Manager."

There are three different required packages for the SDK Manager. The first is SDK Tools, followed by the SDK Platform-tools and SDK Platform. All three of these are required for you to design your application. However, there are other options available for you, so if you want to download all of the content so you can have complete access to everything, you are able to for free. These three program packages include the System Image, which allows you to test out your application on the computer system in a virtual Android based OS. This way, you can see what aspects of the application work, what errors you might run into and what sort of feature is going to be good or bad with your software package. There are other test based services out there, so should you find that you already have one installed on your computer, it is not necessary to use System Image, but it is still a good feature to have.

Android Support is another option that you do not actually need to install. It includes a library with all of the most common issues you might run into, plus instructions on some framework and how to correct certain problems on different mobile phones, as some Android based phones still have overlays on top of the Android operating system that might prove difficult with your application. Lastly, there is the SDK Samples, which give you source code that help you build your application quickly, without having to do it from scratch.

CHAPTER 7- ANDROID EMULATOR AND ANDROID VIRTUAL DEVICE MANAGER

Android Emulator

A lot of people that develop apps for the Android operating system want to be able to have a way to test it. The Android Emulator does just that. To "emulate" means to match by imitation. That's exactly what the Android Emulator is. It's an application that you can run on your computer. The application "pretends" to be an Android phone and developers can test their apps and games using this emulator. This is a great option for developers who want to do an adequate amount of testing of their application before moving it to a physical device. Moving it to a physical device makes it a lot harder to do changes.

The emulator copies all of the software features of an actual physical device. It will display the home screen, app drawer, and applications the exact same way an actual device would. This gives developers a great chance to see exactly how their application would react with an Android device. In addition to that, there are also settings on the emulator that allows you to set certain hardware specifications to see how your application would run. There are a lot of Android phones out there. The hardware from a high-end Android smartphone is going to be very different than the hardware from a lower-end smartphone. This option allows developers to see how their application would run on a range of devices. If an application is only running on high-end hardware specifications, then the developers would have to figure out a way to make their application a little less hardware intensive. Also, there's always the possibility that they would only want their app to be able to run on the latest and greatest hardware. Either way, developers get a chance to see how their application would fare on multiple devices.

In addition to allowing developers to set hardware specifications, the emulator also allows developers to set software specifications. Developers can see how their app would look and run on all the different versions of Android: Froyo all the way through KitKat. There are also ways to set skins to see how your app is going to jive with certain software additions. This means that developers can see how their phone would run on an HTC One vs. a Samsung Galaxy S4. Since Android is such a huge operating system and there are so many variations from device to device, using the emulator is practically a must for those that want to ensure that their app doesn't launch with a variety of problems.

All in all, the Android Emulator is an extremely valuable tool for all of those that want to develop applications and games on the Android operating system. The Android Emulator allows developers to see how their application would run on a base, Google device such as a Nexus. It also gives developers the ability to set hardware and software specifications. This is equivalent of being able to test applications on multiple devices. The Android Emulator is a great piece of software for all Android developers.

Android Virtual Device Manager

What exactly is the Android Device Manager? It's an application that is already running on your Android phone. What it does is it lets you test applications without having to use an actual device. This is something that hooks up to your pc and it operates right there. That way when you go around testing an application, you can do it right from your home computer or pc.

Some of the hardware that this application supports are things like CPU and ARM. This Android virtual device manager can even support a 16-bit LCD screen. It can also work with something like a flash-card memory or most any type of SIMS card.

So how does one create one of these virtual devices from the Android? It's pretty easy to do. The first thing you need to do is install the Android SDK to your mobile device. Wondering how to do this? Simply Google the keyword and look for one of the links that will allow you to install the SDK unit. The links are easy to find and there are so many out there. But you may want to read about what your system requirements are for the SDK unit. Depending on the width band size, some systems may not be able to hold it. So find the link and width band size that your system can adjust to and download and install.

Once this is all downloaded, you will have to open up the task bar and the menu within the SDK. It should be on the right side, most of them are. Click on the AVD's menu on the side of the tool bar. The Android device manager will open from here and you can start to create your own virtual device manager. Start by click the new button. When creating the file, there are a few things that are needed to fill out.

Under the name, you don't need anything there. Under the target portion, pick something from the drop down menu. If there is nothing there, not even the menu button, it means you didn't install it. Or maybe you did, but it wasn't installed properly. If this happens, you will need to go back in and install it once more. The SD card should be a virtual card. The skin section is the screen size for your Android virtual device manager.

Once this is all in, click the create button. Your Android virtual device manager should be one of the top first things on the drop down menu list. All you do is click the start button. And then once a new screen pops up, all you do is hit the launch button and you are all set.

It's really that simple. And this virtual device manager can be taken anywhere with you. It will let you test things from your mobile device, without having to be attached to a computer. Go online and find out more. This way you too can have your own device manager.

CHAPTER 8- ANDROID MANIFEST FILE AND ANDROID MANIFEST EDITOR

The world has become very complicated with many different software, hardware and technology platforms needing to communicate with one another to function properly. Google has seen the underpinnings of the World Wide Web and is expanding its technology for interoperability with any application. This is how the Android Manifest File and Android Manifest Editor assist with this interoperability.

Google Knows Applications

Google has leveraged the knowledge it has gained with its search engines to deliver the Android operating system. Users can download Android Apps on Google Play. For each application, there must be both a root system of instructions for how Google must communicate with it.

With the introduction of Google version 1.8, the comments and suggestions of Web developers have been incorporated into the system. Once a development is stable, it can create more options for customization. Programmers and developers have a wide range of functionality needs for using the Android with new applications.

Android Manifest File in Root Directory

Before a famous actor, athlete or politician gives a speech, there is someone to introduce him. The Android Manifest File performs this function for an application running on the Android operating system. This establishes the parameters for how the application will run. It is generated automatically.

The "AndroidManifest.xml" file is located in the root directory and assists with interoperability. The root directory is basically the unchanging blueprint of your Android system. It creates the standards for your system.

The Android Manifest File names the application Java package along with describing the components, capabilities and conditions thereof. This file creates the icons and declares the permissions for access to the application programming interface (API). This Manifest file sets rules and guidelines to make the application and system function properly and efficiently together: Elements, Attributes, Classes, Values and Libraries.

What is the Android Manifest Editor?

Now what if you are a Web developer and want to customize how an application is run for Android? This could include display, color or permission options. You don't want to rewrite the entire code for the Android Manifest File every time, do you? No.

Before version 1.8, the only choice available for customizing the Manifest was to check the "Do now write manifest file" option. But that was like throwing out the baby with the bathwater. With version 1.8, you can use the Android Manifest Editor tool to add, remove or update the Manifest File. Use these commands - Add/Remove Text, Set Attribute, Add Replacement or Add/Remove Permission.

Professionals may want to tweak a certain attribute for an application. When the Manifest File is created, it will overwrite this feature with the original settings. The editor can be used to create a "customized" manifest for the application.

"AddManifestText" will direct the system to add the desired computer code whenever the Manifest File is generated. This saves time "rewriting" the code every time the application is compiled. Experts create these advanced features and save them for future use.

About The Author

Jason Hunter has been working in the field of technology for years and he is always looking out for the next big development in the field. In the last few years with the further development of Smartphones and tablets, android development has come to the fore. He spent a lot of time doing research and eventually ended up doing android development in addition to his other duties.

The purpose of his book is to let the reader know that it is not as difficult as it seems. If you have a love for all things technology, then you will be able to learn about the latest trends in android development with ease.

www.ingramcontent.com/pod-product-compliance
Lightning Source LLC
Chambersburg PA
CBHW070928050326
40689CB00015B/3661